PERFECTLY IMPERFECT

A Collection of Poetry

By:

Jennifer L. Gibaldi

1st Edition

ISBN 979-8-9850793-3-3 (PRINT)

ISBN 979-8-9850793-4-0 (EBOOK)

Contents

Ready for the World

Such a tender round face,
With the most perfect little button nose.
A joy to welcome to the family.

Someone who wasn't supposed to be,
Is a new treasure who doesn't make a peep.
No one minds when she is around.

She loves to dance,
She loves to sing.
Anything to do with music.

She hides her more artistic side.
Writing, drawing.
Anything to express herself.

Finally, she is broken out of her shell,
Showing her work to others.
She accepts the praise.

Now she is a young woman,
Almost out of high school.
Will she reach her goals in life?

She has been through a lot already,
So, no surprises can await her.
She is ready for what the world has to offer.

Life is but a Circle

Fun, carefree, filled with love, warmth.
Lonely, shy, filled with anxiety, doubts.
Laughter, joy, filled with memories, confidence.
Stress, shame, filled with insults, insecurities.
Relief, knowledge, filled with growth, reinvention.
Overcoming obstacles shapes who we are.

If Only They Knew

A pretty smile that lights up the room,
Kind eyes that open her soul.
A warm embrace that melts your heart,
A gentle touch that calms your nerves.
Kind words to ease your fears.
She has a way of making those around her feel loved.
A way of making them feel safe, protected.
If only they knew.
If only they knew the frown behind her smile.
The sadness in those kind eyes.
The desire to be hugged back.
If only they knew the loneliness behind the gentle touch.
The hurt behind those kind words.
She takes on the weight of the world,
So those around her don't have to.
But who takes on the weight of the world for her?

Mirror

"What do you see?" He whispers quietly.
Long, flowing golden brown curls.
Kind, caring brown eyes.
Warm, inviting smile.
A heart filled with love.
"What do you see?" He whispers again.
A sea of gray that surrounds the face.
Tired, sad eyes.
Lines that frame a frown.
A heart that has been broken more than once.
"What do you see?" He whispers.
A kind soul.
Thoughtful, caring, sincere.
Understanding and compassionate.
A woman who would fight the world for you.
"What do you see?" He whispers one last time.
A troubled soul.
Scared, anxious, alone.
Tired and unworthy.
A girl who watches the world pass her by.
She looks away from the mirror,
Tears in her eyes and responds:
"I see me."

A Special Word

As I lay in bed at night,
And think of all things I have,
Not once do I think of you.

I try not to let thoughts of you enter my mind,
But sometimes they slip in
As I sit back and watch the rest of the world.

As I watch them in their glory,
And as I watch them celebrate their happiness,
I realize I am jealous.

I'm jealous of who they are,
Jealous of what they have.
Because what they have is what I want
And I've come to realize that what I want is you.

I want you to be there when I come home late at night.
You are the one I want there with open arms when something bad happens,
And you are the one I want there when something good happens.

When I think of everything you missed in the past,
And all the things you will miss in the future,
It upsets me greatly.

It hurts me deeply to think of you,
Out there with them,
Instead of here with me.

All I want in life is to know you.
Unfortunately, it looks like I'm not going to get that chance.
At least not this time around.

The Long Walk

Tan with a hint of red,
Only one person can fit.
Colorful flowers lined along the edge,
Floating candles in tall, elegant stands.
A trellis with tiny white lights,
Entwined with rose vines.
A wooden gazebo sits alone at the end,
With the most exquisite crystal chandelier.
A tall, well-built man is standing alone,
Beckoning you in.
Though you have never seen him before,
You feel as though you know him.
As you approach, he smiles sweetly,
And it is like watching the sunrise.
You place your hand in his,
And you feel reassured.
The feeling of being alone in the world disappears,
And you are overcome with unconditional love.
You feel as though you have met,
But you know that is impossible.
As you step into the gazebo,
The words ring in your ears for an eternity:
"Welcome home, daughter."

As Our Paths Cross

Just as I begin to think I am moving on,
My life takes an unexpected turn.
As I follow the bend,
My life turns into chaos,
And nothing is as it should be.

Just as I begin to think I have everything figured out,
My world gets turned upside down.
As I start to turn with it,
My world becomes disheveled,
And nothing is as it should be.

Just as I begin to think I am happy,
My emotions start twisting around.
As my heart twists with it,
My soul gets tied in a knot,
And nothing is as it should be.

Just as I think I have forgotten,
It seems fate has other plans.
For at the end of every side of the world,
And at every point in a twist-
Our paths seem to cross yet again.

Broken

I had it all figured out,
What I wanted my life to be.
I knew exactly what I would tolerate,
And what I wouldn't.
I knew my worth,
And what I deserved.
I had confidence,
And knew what I had to offer the world.

It didn't happen all at once,
But rather slowly over time.
The view of my life changed,
What I wanted was no longer clear.
I became a shattered soul,
An empty shell of myself.

My worthiness became ineptness,
I no longer felt deserving.
I stopped talking,
I stopped smiling,
I stopped being me.
How had I let myself become something I swore I never would?

Lost On the Wrong Path

How can you find yourself,
If you didn't even know you were lost?
You go through your days habitually,
Like a robot on autopilot.
Until one morning, you look in the mirror.
When did you become so old?
Your once bright and lively eyes,
Now have lines and are tired.
Your beautiful smile that used to light up the room,
Now hangs in a perpetual frown.
Your thick dark curls that used to hang loose around your face,
Are now turning silver and hiding in a bun.
You no longer recognize the woman staring back.
This can't be you; it must be a stranger.
You continue to stare, questions building in your mind.
When did you stop smiling?
What happened to the light in your eyes?
How come you stopped wearing your hair down?
So many questions, with only one answer:
You lost yourself following the wrong path.

He Didn't Mean It

It was my fault,
He didn't mean it.
I knew he had a long day at work and was tired.
I should have waited for a better moment to say something.

It was my fault,
He didn't mean it.
I provoked him-
Sometimes I just don't know when to stop.

It was my fault,
He didn't mean it.
What was I thinking about, going out in a dress like that?
Of course I was going to get looks and attention.

It was my fault,
He didn't mean it.
I should have checked with him before going out with friends-
What if he needed me?

I tried to live my life, have some fun.
I should have known better,
But I don't need to worry anymore.
I know he didn't mean it,
He couldn't help himself.
It was all my fault.

Because of You

I look up and see vacant eyes.
Sad eyes,
A lost soul.
And my mind wonders,
Is it because of you?

I look up and see vibrant eyes.
Determined eyes,
A feeling of pride.
And my mind wonders,
Is it because of you?

I look up and see self-doubt.
Second guessing every decision,
Faltering on every thought.
And my mind wonders,
Is it because of you?

I look up and see fearlessness.
Confidence in every decision.
Intent behind every move.
And my mind wonders,
Is it because of you?

I look up and see reflection.
The lost soul who found pride.
The self-doubt who found confidence.
And my mind knows,
It is all because of you.

No Escape

I thought I left.
I packed my bags.
I took her stuff.
We got in the truck and drove away.
I thought I left.
Phone calls to find out where she was,
Threats of calling the police.
Nights of anxiety and crying.
I thought I left.
Voicemails of screaming and cursing.
Showing up at my job,
Random pictures of my car sent to my phone.
I thought I left.
Hearing a voice that sounds like yours.
A word or phrase you always used.
Driving by your old street,
Seeing a truck that looks like yours.
I thought I left,
But now I know-
There is no escaping you.
You have embedded yourself so deep in my mind,
You consume every bit of me.
Every thought,
Every worry,
Every fear.
How can I make you go away?
How do I take my life back?

Trapped

Confined,
Trapped,
Unable to escape.
I look around me to find nothing but darkness.
No windows,
No light,
Only shadows.
In the distance I can hear voices.
I open my mouth to scream but no sound comes out.
My eyes close.
My breath catches.
My heart skips a beat and my mind races.
How did I get here?
How will I get out?
Will anyone even notice I am gone?
I try to feel around me,
But I can't move my arms.
I try to kick,
But my legs feel like they are covered with lead.
My eyes close tighter as the tears start to fall.
Confined,
Trapped,
Unable to escape.

Powerful Words

You're lucky I stayed, anyone else would have left.
I don't want her, but I have no choice.
I am waiting for you to get fed up with my nonsense,
And leave me.
Who is going to want to you now?
You come with too much baggage.
What you are looking for does not exist.

These are the words spoken by a man who does not truly Love you, even though he says he does.
A man with insecurities who is intimidated by your worth.
A man who feels the need to break you down,
So you won't escape.

I am here for you, but you need to let me help.
We will get through this together.
Tell me your dreams, we will figure out a way.
You always underestimate yourself.
I wish you would see yourself the way others see you.
The way I see you.
Determined.
Talented.
Smart.
Knowledgeable.
Dedicated.
Beautiful.

These are the words spoken by a man who truly loves you with every fiber of his being.
A man who wants you to remember how valuable,
And special you are to this world.

Always My Savior

"Come with me," he whispers quietly.
As his hand gently touches mine,
My gaze moves to him slowly.
My breath catches in my throat,
Tears form in my weary eyes.
My hands begin to tremble slightly,
And I wonder if he notices.
"Come with me," he whispers again.
His hand against my pale cheek,
I lean my forehead against his.
Placing my hand on his chest,
I close my eyes and inhale deeply.
He gently wipes away a tear.
"Come with me," he whispers louder.
I know he genuinely loves me,
Will always be there for me.
I can feel safe with him,
Let my guard down, be me.
"Come with me," he says softly.
I take his hands in mine,
Wrap each arm around my back.
Leaning my head on his chest,
I whisper ever so softly, "Always."

My Dear Angel

"I'm sorry", I hear in the distance.
"There's no heartbeat", while my own is racing.
Somewhere, a door slams and my breath catches.
"These things just happen."
My eyes search the room, but I don't see him.
He is gone.
Everything becomes blurry.
"There is no explanation."
My hands cradle my stomach.
"We'll call ahead, let them know you are coming."
I look up and my gaze meets the doctor's eyes.
My face is wet with the overflow of tears.
I feel arms around me, but not the ones I need.
"I really am so sorry", as the nurse helps me off the table.
The tears start to come faster, harder.
My knees feel weak.
I can't stop shaking.
I look down, still cradling my stomach,
Cradling you.
I fall against the nurse, and I cry.
I cry for the nine months I got to feel your every move.
I cry for the lifetime we will never get to have.
My baby,
My daughter,
My Angel.

My Miracle

Although you had not officially entered the world yet,
You let yourself be known.
Strong.
Playful.
A force to be reckoned with.
Then you were here.
Sweet, perfect little round face.
Pudgy cheeks with the tiniest little mouth.
Four words changed our lives that day:
"She has Down syndrome".
Then you were placed in my arms.
It didn't matter that the unexpected had happened.
That the life I had envisioned for us would not come to be.
I took one look at you and my heart melted.
We would make a new path,
A different path.
Sure, there would be more obstacles,
But always the same outcome.
Love.
Family.
Growth.
Lessons.
You helped me to slow down and live.
To take the time to see the beauty in all the small things.
You have been my daily inspiration with your kindness.
Your determination.
Your strength.
Yes, our path changed the day you were born-
I got a much better one instead.

My Daughter

The warmth of your tiny fingers against my neck.
The soft flutter of your heartbeat against my chest.
The sweet smell of fresh baby powder as your hair tickles my chin.
I close my eyes and try to remember.

The sound of your infectious giggles.
The way your eyes light up when you smile.
The sweet sound of your voice when you squeal with excitement.
I close my eyes and try to remember.

I try to remember that tiny little life that relied on me to keep her safe.
That innocent little girl who found joy in everything around her.
That sweet little girl who copied everything I did,
Wanting to be "just like Mommy".
But I can't keep my eyes closed forever,
I know I need to open them.

I need to open them and see you now.
How nurturing and caring you have become.
Your confidence and determination.
How proud you are of your independence.
I see you.
I see all of you.

I see the fragile new life who looked to me for guidance.
I see the amazing young woman who is now ready to guide herself.
And I am honored and proud to be called your mom.

16

16 years of warm embraces,
Your arms wrapping around me as I hear "I love you Mom".
Sharing stories of my own heartaches as I wipe away the tears from yours.
16 years of secret glances and shared jokes.
The rolling of the eyes and slight smirk when I do that "corny Mom thing".
16 years of watching you and your sister bond.
Taking care of each other,
Loving each other.
16 years of watching you learn and grow.
Trying to find your own way,
Become your own being.
I was robbed of 16 joyful, beautiful years.
Instead, I had 16 years of missing out.
Of wondering and dreaming.
16 years of wondering what you would look like.
Would you and your sister get along?
Or would you view her as a burden?
Would we be close?
Or would you hide in your room to avoid me?
16 years of never being able to hold you,
Hug you,
Comfort you.
Tell you "I love you".
16 years of lost memories.
16 years since I got to hold you for both the first and last time,
16 years since I kissed you good-bye.
Happy Sweet 16 my dear sweet Angel.

Guardian Angels

My heart shattered into a million pieces,
My world completely upside down-
Life was just not the same.
How could I possibly go on?

Her sweet little innocent face,
That lit up the room when she smiled-
Needed my love and attention.
How could I ignore her?

Such a lonely feeling,
Nothing but emptiness inside-
Living with guilt.
Did I cause this?

Her tiny little arms reaching out for me,
Her pudgy little fingers caressing my cheeks-
My heart melts with her snuggles.
How could I not hug her back?

Just when my world ended and I felt like life was over,
She was there to keep me going.
When I was wracked with guilt and thought it was my fault,
She was there to prove I was doing it right.

Losing you forced me to open my eyes,
And see my life for what it really was.
Losing you encouraged me to think,
About what lessons I wanted her to learn.
Losing you gave me strength,
To walk away and start over.

She is my Guardian Angel here on Earth,
You are my Guardian Angel up in Heaven.
And I am forever lucky and grateful to have you both.

In The Words of a Flame

And who art thou? Said I to the deep burning fire.
His answer:
I am the desire of destruction.
I come to destroy, said the voice of the flames.
People often underestimate me.
Enticing me to show my strength.
But when I do-
They fear me.
Why is that? he asked in a rage.
Not liking my silence,
He grew angry:
I have the power to make people fear me – I choose what I destroy.
(And I often like to watch those who fear me, as they suffer from my heat.)

The First One

Waiting-
For me to fail,
To follow in the footsteps of those that came before me.
Judging-
My every move, every decision.
Never thinking that I would be strong enough, determined enough to be the first.
The first one to graduate High School,
To go to college.
The first one to stand up for myself,
To declare that I am worthy and demand that others acknowledge it too.
The first one willing to be alone if it means having full control over my life again.
The first one to challenge you.
To challenge your thoughts, your perception of me.
Your judgements and your negative views.
I am the first one,
And I am worth it!

Good Enough for Me

How do I prove myself to you?
I get straight A's and make honor roll every quarter.
I participate in job programs through-out high school,
Gaining experience in different fields.
I proudly graduate, despite some health obstacles,
Yet it doesn't seem to be good enough.

I work full time and attend college,
Studying while picking up extra shifts.
I find my own transportation to both work and school,
And pay all my own bills, including for my wedding.
Yet it doesn't seem to be good enough.

I raise my daughter alone,
Putting her before anything else.
I walk away from a bad situation with practically nothing,
In order to make a better life for her.
Yet it doesn't seem to be good enough.

Why?
Why am I trying to prove myself to you?
Why does it matter what you think?
It shouldn't.

I graduated high school and went to college.
I worked hard to pay my own way and not rely on others.
I ensured a safe, secure and loving environment for my child.
That is what matters.
And that is good enough for me.

Perfect Mess

This is me.
All of me.
I am a perfect mess.
I live in organized chaos.
My kitchen table has piles of papers, bags and boxes.
The stuffed chicken recipe you need?
4th or 5th paper down in the pile on the left by the stove...
I cry at commercials and laugh until I snort.
I get defensive when asked questions.
My voice has a permanent tone of sarcasm and attitude.
My outward appearance is sophisticated, classy, feminine.
My sense of humor is that of a 12-year-old boy.
I have long beautiful curls that are frizzy as hell.
My smile is warm and soft, with a chipped front tooth.
I am a responsible adult who is just a kid at heart.
I go to work every day, putting forth 100% effort in every task,
Then come home and make fart jokes.
I raised a beautiful young woman,
Who I love to tease and annoy.
I love my husband with all my heart,
But sometimes hold back on the affection I show.
This is me.
All of me.
I am a perfect mess.

About the Author

Jennifer Gibaldi is a new and upcoming poet, writer, and author. She discovered and fell in love with the world of literature at an early age. Finding comfort in her books, she writes with heart and passion, drawing on her real-life experiences for inspiration.

Nothing is more important to Jennifer than her family. She is the proud wife of a volunteer firefighter and mother to a beautiful young woman with Down syndrome. She cherishes every second she gets to spend with them.

Jennifer is grateful for the ongoing support she has received throughout the years from her family and friends. She knows how fortunate and lucky she is to have them and can't imagine having gone through some of her life challenges without them.

Jennifer hopes that through her writing and sharing her stories, she'll be able to help others to see themselves in a new light. She hopes you have enjoyed taking this little trip with her and can't wait to share the next adventure with you!

www.ingramcontent.com/pod-product-compliance
Lightning Source LLC
LaVergne TN
LVHW010550100826
845148LV00013B/2676
* 9 7 9 8 9 8 5 0 7 9 3 3 3 *